Lottie Moon

What do you need?

The true story of Lottie Moon and the Christmas Offering

Catherine Mackenzie
Illustrated by Rita Ammassari

Lottie Moon lived in America. She had dark hair, and sparkly brown eyes. She was clever and fun. Her friends and family loved her.

But sometimes Lottie tried to skip church. Even though her father had died before she was thirteen years old, Lottie gave no thought to her own life or death.

Sometimes Lottie
tried to skip church.

One day, however, Lottie went to a revival meeting. Revival meetings are where people gather together to hear about God's forgiveness. Lottie thought that the meeting might give her more ideas about how to tease her Christian friends.

However, when she was there, everything the preacher said made sense. Her conscience started to bother her and that night Lottie asked God to forgive her sins. From that day, Lottie never skipped church!

Lottie asked God to forgive her sins.

Lottie left school at a difficult time in America. There was a civil war and Lottie helped in the army hospitals. When the war was over, Lottie had to find a job. She wasn't a little rich girl anymore.

She taught children from poor families, particularly girls, but then Lottie felt that God was calling her to work as a missionary in China.

Lottie taught children from poor families.

Lottie was good at languages and so, in 1873, when she was thirty-three years old, she boarded a ship in San Francisco bound for China. She was going to work as a missionary for the Southern Baptists.

First of all she taught children, but eventually she became a full-time evangelist in P'ingtu and Hwangshien. Many in those areas came to trust in Christ.

Lottie boarded a ship bound for China.

She went to stay in a town called P'ingtu because the people there were eager to find God.

In order to help the Chinese people feel more at home with her, Lottie decided to wear the same kind of clothes as they wore. With her hair done up in a bun, Lottie looked just like a Chinese woman. She realised that when she became more like the Chinese, they showed her more respect. Lottie was showing the Chinese how much she loved them and how much God loved them too.

Lottie looked just like a Chinese woman.

Lottie spent so much time nursing others, she became known as 'The Mother of North China'. Many missionaries fell ill and had to return home, some even died.

Lottie wrote letters to the church at home asking Christians in the United States to send more workers to China and to send financial support too. There was so much need. Lottie especially asked the women of the churches to raise funds at Christmas time. 'Do you really believe it is more blessed to give than to receive?' she asked.

Lottie wrote letters to the church at home.

Great persecution came to China. When Lottie heard that one of the Christians in Sha-ling had been seized, she set off to see what she could do.

She found the man tied to a post and bleeding. Lottie was so angry. She was small, but she pushed her way through the crowd and stood between them and the elderly Christian.

'If you try to destroy this church, you'll have to kill me first. Jesus gave himself for Christians. Now I am ready to die for him.' The crowd drifted away. 'Our Master, Jesus, always watches over us. He meets our needs,' Lottie told the other Christians.

Lottie was so angry.

After having spent some time in America, speaking to the church there about the mission, Lottie returned to China. However, the country was at war with Japan. More trouble came in 1900 when the Chinese government began to support an anti-Christian group called the Boxers. The Boxers hated Christians and they robbed and vandalised businesses.

Some Christians at P'ingtu were thrown in jail – so a message was sent to Lottie begging for help. But if Lottie travelled to P'ingtu, the Boxers were bound to discover her. It would not be safe.

The Boxers hated Christians.

However, Lottie hatched a plan. A friend gave her a special government carriage called a 'shentze'. She then dressed up as a government official. All along the route the Boxers bowed in respect, not knowing who was really in the carriage. When she arrived at P'ingtu, Lottie was able to help the believers.

Lottie eventually left for Japan, but returned to work in China for a while. She paid one more visit to America, which was her last.

The Boxers bowed in respect.

In 1911 revolution broke out in China and there was severe unrest. All the missionaries from Hwanghsien were evacuated. When Lottie heard of this, she said to herself, 'I am needed in Hwanghsien.' When the missionaries returned, they were surprised to find everything running smoothly. Lottie then announced that she was heading back to Tengchow, even though there was a battle going on.

Nobody could persuade her to stay. So, urgent messages were sent to contacts on both sides of the conflict. When she arrived, both generals laid down their arms until she had passed through.

Lottie said to herself, 'I am needed.'

Lottie often put the needs of others before her own. Eventually, she became very sick.

On Christmas Eve, 1912, as she was on board a ship in the port of Kobe, Japan, Lottie Moon died. She was seventy-two years old.

A monument was erected to her memory in the Chinese town of Tengchow. But perhaps the greatest memorial to her is the Christmas offering that is taken up in Southern Baptist churches each December. The Lottie Moon Christmas Offering is still making a difference – bringing the good news of Christ to the world.

The Lottie Moon Christmas Offering is still making a difference.

This book is in memory of Jackie and Elma Ross, examples of faith in truth and practice.

10 9 8 7 6 5 4 3 2 1
Copyright © 2015 Catherine Mackenzie
ISBN: 978-1-78191-588-2
Published by Christian Focus Publications,
Geanies House, Fearn, Tain, Ross-shire, IV20 1TW, Scotland, U.K.
www.christianfocus.com

Cover design by Daniel van Straaten
Printed in China

All titles in this series:
1. Amy Carmichael: Can brown eyes be made blue? 978-1-84550-108-2
2. Hudson Taylor: Could somebody pass the salt? 978-1-84550-111-2
3. Corrie ten Boom: Are all of the watches safe? 978-1-84550-109-9
4. George Müller: Does money grow on trees? 978-1-84550-110-5
5. Helen Roseveare: What's in the parcel? 978-1-84550-383-3
6. David Livingstone: Who is the bravest? 978-1-84550-384-0
7. John Calvin: What is the Truth? 978-1-84550-560-8
8. Martin Luther:What should I do? 978-1-84550-561-5
9. Eric Liddell: Are you ready? 978-1-84550-790-9
10. Mary Slessor: What is it like? 978-1-84550-791-6
11. C.S. Lewis: Can you imagine? 978-1-78191-160-0
12. Gladys Aylward: Are you going to stop? 978-1-78191-161-7
13. Lottie Moon: What do you need? 978-1-78191-588-2
14. John Knox: Who will save you? 978-1-78191-587-5